# About Love & Fate

Raquel Brown

Presentation by *BookLeaf Publishing*

Web: www.bookleafpub.com

E-mail: info@bookleafpub.com

ISBN: 9789395756303

First edition 2022

# DEDICATION

For anyone who is lost in thoughts of love

For anyone who is caught between fate and reality,

And a reminder to love yourself effortlessly.

# ACKNOWLEDGEMENT

Having lost the desire to write, I am grateful to God for restoring my passion. A special thank you goes out to my English teachers throughout my primary, secondary and university years, who never stopped believing in me, as well as my family and friends who have always listened to my poetry and encouraged me to keep on writing.

# PREFACE

I chose the topic of love and fate, as in my childhood, I was fascinated by the concept of romance, and one of the first poems that sparked my love of poetry was 'Porphyria's Lover' by Robert Browning. This poem was given to me in class by a teacher, and after that, I began creating poetry.

Writing these poems was like being reacquainted with an old friend, as I realised I had neglected this part of myself for far too long, and initially, I struggled. My first poem, like the first pancake you bake, is never exactly right, but the one after that is so much better, and yes, my first pancake poem is included. I'm curious as to whether you noticed it!

Naturally, you'll discover traces of me in the poems; though some of these poems were not inspired by actual occurrences, it was the emphasis and feeling I was focused on, and I wanted to write from the heart.

# Love's Eyes

Through the eyes of Love
Your flaws will remain hidden
You are protected

# While You Keep Me Waiting

While you keep me waiting
Pinching bruised ends of paper
You've left me at the height of feeling
Too afraid, and reluctant to let go
Immersed inside a story
A book without an ending

While you keep me waiting
There is something you should know,
Parts of me are missing
Curiouser and curiouser
Is there no desire to go deeper?

For beneath it all,
You'll find someone who's hurting
Someone who's healing,
Someone too precious for revealing

# You Carved Me In Heaven

Beauty from the beginning
In perfect light, I dwelt
You carved me in heaven
It's no surprise I fell

Incapable of caveating your affection
Your love unassailable, unquestionable
Desire spread, more compelling, daring
Of which, in your field of vision
I could see, you were half-impaired

To preclude your judgement
My silence became incumbent
Notwithstanding, my devotion
My passion and amity
I had to set me free
To share with you,
The parts that made me, me

# A Sense of Self-Love

Do you know what it means to me?

To have a peace that's undisrupted
A quiet place, a safe space
That's warm and gives you comfort
To be able to take a minute and breathe
To let your thoughts and feelings
Run wild, run free

To have a second undisturbed
A sense of calm, an opportunity for reflection
A closed-off space
A private heaven
Just for you, where no one enters

To be able to tap into your senses
To enter a world of creativity
To see the moment through different lenses
To know that I'm enough, I'm worthy

I've built myself the perfect place
I've entered a domain of harmony
Where there is no more than me

# Love is your Rose

5

Love yourself, for you are delicate
Like a blooming red red rose
You need the space to grow
And the time to reveal your inner beauty

Love is necessary when it is nourished
With the kindness of words and affirmation
Carry yourself with a vision of confidence
And open yourself up to the belief that anything
can happen.

# For The Sake Of Love

For the sake of love
You're giving up your energy
For the sake of love
You'll become someone else
Someone else, entirely

You'll deny yourself healing and affection
You used to love your independence
Look at what's become of you
You're missing out
You're holding out for a sheet of paper
For some sweet novel
For some sweet story

For the sake of love
I implore you to see yourself
Let me be your reflection
For inside you, there is something Invaluable
If only you could see
And hold it close, so dear

# The Muse in Myself

I wrote a note to myself
Just jotted dots of broken thought
Feelings parading behind
Words my heart evoked

What had been locked up
I sought to retrieve
For when I opened the book
I discovered the muse
Smiling...
Staring back at me

# The Season of Love

Breathing with the breeze
We amplified our senses
Before nightfall we reached our peak
Not ready for the sundown
Whilst our love spun us into infinity
Our passion was all-consuming

We burnt the tips of our wings
We dipped them in ice
We burnt once for love
For us, we burnt twice

After light, our love burnt out
And Like bullet pelts, the rain poured down
My heart rolled on the thunder
Filling the air with a shrill-tinged cry
The angels wept in silence

It took from me a swift retreat
My mind reticent with falling memories
With everything changing
Everything passed
Everything froze but dust on glass

# A Not So Quiet Crush

My eyes were piqued, ablaze with sparks
Advertent eyes were upon me,
A flush of heat cut through my heart
In the hopes that I'd endear,
In that moment, I built the tension
A silent pause… a vacant stare
One that words could not repair

Just one touch of his eyes
Left me shook, and misaligned,
Sweeping heat against my cheeks
Sweat between my chest and thighs
Just one bait of his breath,
My tongue-in-cheek
He laughed, in Jest

# The Pedantic Side of Love

It's the meticulous attention to detail
The double-checks,
The triple-checks,
The build-up, the anticipation
A quiet stillness, that renders muteness
Despite, the chaos of the sound
Even when there's a chance to speak
Lips become benumbed

# Something More Than Conversation

It was relayed back and forth
This free-form discussion
To each our own
We held our tongues
Trying to decipher what had happened

There were many parts that grabbed us
That left us on the periphery of our seats
Forgetting, or not paying attention
To all the anomalies,
Whilst digressing,
The conversation changed direction

I said some things
I swear, I meant it
Still, I couldn't talk to you
And If our premise was love,
Our goal was for love to last forever.

# Of Fate and Autumn

September brought with it a familiar smell
Books marked with yellow pages
Tables stained with rings of gold and brown
Amber lights, entwined, embracing
A honeyed hue of green abstains
Shifting side-to-side
Holding out for summers gape
Brimming with broken half-empty sighs
As the Piano plays its somber sounds
And falling leaves adorn the ground
Wheeling, weaving, whirling
Destiny's wheel still turning
As the light retraces, the lips, they curl,
And as hope retreats, so does our place in time

# A Desire for Love

My desire is reflected in the nakedness of truth
My truth is concealed by fear and the absence of
love
My feelings are carried in the movement of the
waves

Feel the heaviness of my heart
Anchored, stubborn and unmoving

How I've longed…

To bask in grace's goodness
To bear witness to the expression of love
To be surrounded with peace and serenity
And to be sheltered by loving arms

# A Lovers Request

In the wrong direction, the stars are pointing
Forgive me for not noticing, the cross in our
paths
Forgive me for being intrusive
For what the world denies us
Is surely not what love intended

To reverse what has been ruled
I'll place these words in heaven
And request a sign from God
For I'll wait…
And I'll wait…
For our souls to realign and the stars to be
rewritten

# Underneath Your Shelter

We will share one umbrella
Huddling Forward
Shoulder to shoulder

Through the storms of life
Stopping but for a moment
To fill our empty spaces

I'll love you forever…

For this I am certain
For in you I have found my soulmate

# Elements of Passion

A humm A humm A hummm
Sounds of Autumn
Sunlight shimmering lights
Hope is searching, seeking sight
Colours languish over summer days
Arms move forward
Murmurs Murmurs Murmurs
Breath turning into a sweet release
Stolen moments, passing memories

# Next to Never

By the sun you held my eyes
By the night, I held yours
Two worlds coexisting,
Never colliding
Two worlds searching
Never finding

Ever different
Ever the same

Never in the same place
Never at the right time

# Broken and Unaware

When your thoughts go wandering
And my eyes reach out to your smile
I sit and wait in slumber
Like a rose drenched in water

Still breathing in the moments
As the world around you becomes enchanted
As it brightens, sparkles, and comes to life
Still, I sit in waiting...
Searching for the diamonds in your eyes

I take one timid step toward you
Even with the kind exchange of words
There are many left unspoken
Even then,
I feel you close; yet still so far away

# To Love the Impalpable

You've spent a lot of time in my head
You're not someone I know; you're just someone
I've met
Yet, something feels strange and vaguely
familiar
You're not my friend, yet you're not a stranger
You're evasive to me, yet there in plain sight
I've been hidden from you, but not in the night

I bury my head to drown these feelings inside
There's something special about you
I just don't know why?

Then there are days when I pretend like I'm fine
Then our eyes start to meet

And our souls stop the time

# The Comet

The stars fashion themselves
Into thinly veiled compliments
Bringing with them sweet accents of gold dust
                                        Flickering …
Twinkling…
                              Through… and …
Through
Darkness recedes in the presence
Of sporadic bursts of light
And the eyes are forever reaching
On the edge of falling into forever

The light disappears
As quickly as it enters

And a sense of sadness dims the fire

# After Dark Dreams

Daylight turns purple blending into shades of
blue
Across the sky, the stars shine bright and clear
Their dancing lights spin in aggregation
As satiating sounds becomes love's pioneer

Curled up and crouched before a roaring fire
Indulging in fantasies and possibilities
As I entertain my imagination and creativity
Spending time in the quintessential atmosphere

My mind meditating on the perfect passion
Every day, I wake up without you here
Always and always,
                              I'll dream of you